Hoggy Doggy Meets The Mooch Pooch

By R. Kaye Springer

Hoggy Doggy Meets The Mooch Pooch

By R. Kaye Springer

www.RKayeSpringer.com

© 2021 R. Kaye Springer

All rights reserved. No portion of this book may be reproduced in any form without permission from the publisher, except as permitted by U.S. Copyright law.

ISBN: 978-1-64945-031-9

His friend
The Mooch Pooch
is scruffy and small.

And cute  Really, really cute!

They meet everyday
at the Lark Park to play.

They come with their owners, Max and Shay, who look both ways when they cross the street and hold their dogs' leashes tightly so the dogs don't run away!

But now the dogs are at the park and they can't wait to run and bark!

Me first!

No, me!

They chase bouncy squirrels.

Oh no!
Are they back again?

What can I do to get rid of them?

I know what!
I'll bean them with a nut!

They bark at chirpy birds.

What can I do to get rid of these two?

I know what!
I'll poop on their heads!

They find big trees
to pee on -
but it won't be
on this one !

So can we pee
on the sign ?

I AM A
NO DOGPEE
TREE

Why doesn't she mind getting dragged behind?

Because Hoggy Doggy does all the tugging.

Mooch Pooch slides behind and enjoys the ride!

Then Hoggy Doggy and Mooch Pooch wrestle.
They just nip.
They don't get hurt.

Anyway, it rained yesterday,
so now they're covered in dirt.

Oh no! There's barking and flying earth near the fence down by the lake.

What have they gotten into now?

What did they find
to make such
a row?
No, it's not
a bitey snake

Hey, you meanies!

Leave me alone!

This is my home!

or a chipmunk

I'll run up and down and around this tree until they get dizzy and go away!

or a gopher.

I've been underground all day. I'll just kick some dirt their way!

It's a mud turtle
trying to tuck
his head
inside
his shell
so the dogs
can't bite him -
and he's frightened,
you can tell.

Now their owners,
Max and Shay
must run fast
to save the day.

They put on their
Turtle Hero capes
and carry him
away.

They're glad the turtle
wasn't bitten
and they're glad
he's not a snake.

They take the
frightened turtle home
and dump him
in the lake.

The dogs want to know where did their smelly chew toy go?

What?

They took it away?

They'll be sorry! We'll howl all day!

But now it's time
to walk back home,
clean up
their muddy tracks,
gobble down
their dinners,
and start
SNEAKING
SNACKS !

Hurry ! Yummy ! Mine ! NO Mine!

Look for
"Hoggy Doggy Sneaks Snacks"
and other
R. Kaye Springer books
available on
Amazon.

All R. Kaye Springer
illustrations
are done with markers
and colored pencils.

Artists use all kinds of tools
besides computers!

Made in the USA
Coppell, TX
14 October 2021

This is Hoggy Doggy.

He is tall and round as a ball.

Hoggy Doggy Meets The Mooch Pooch

By R. Kaye Springer